THRILLING SCIENCE AND TECHNOLOGY JOBS

ASTRONAUTS

Ruth Owen and John Willis

AV2

Step 1
Go to www.av2books.com

Step 2
Enter this unique code
ASJNLY5GM

Step 3
Explore your interactive eBook!

CONTENTS
- 4 Just Another Day at Work
- 6 The International Space Station
- 8 Astronaut Training
- 10 Training for Zero Gravity
- 12 Welcome to the Space Station
- 14 Life on the Space Station
- 16 Sleeping, Running, and . . .
- 18 Astronaut Scientists at Work
- 20 A Human Experiment
- 22 Ready to Spacewalk
- 24 Walking in Space
- 26 The Journey Home
- 28 Welcome Back to Earth
- 29 Historic Space Missions
- 30 Astronaut Quiz
- 31 Key Words/Index

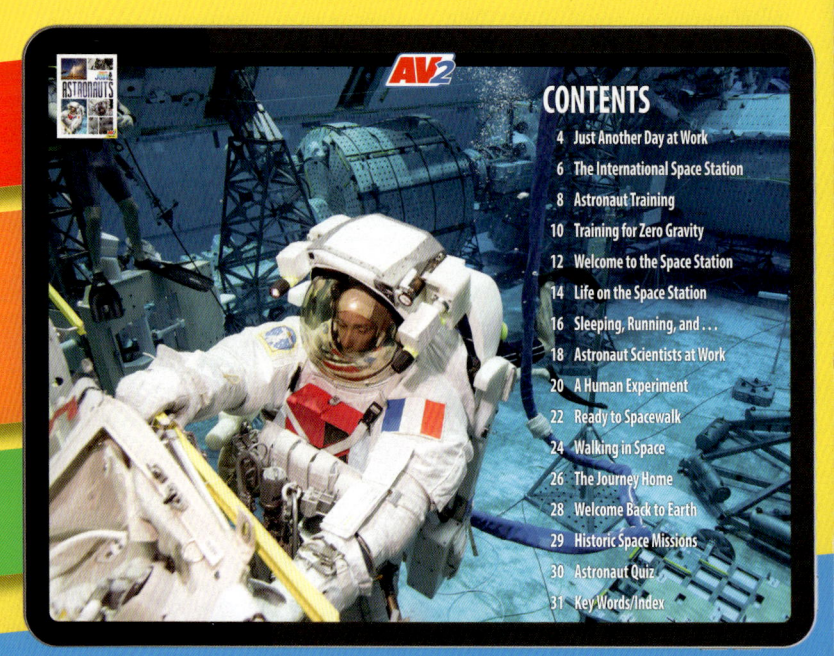

AV2 is optimized for use on any device

Your interactive eBook comes with...

Contents
Browse a live contents page to easily navigate through resources

Audio
Listen to sections of the book read aloud

Videos
Watch informative video clips

Weblinks
Gain additional information for research

Try This!
Complete activities and hands-on experiments

Key Words
Study vocabulary, and complete a matching word activity

Quizzes
Test your knowledge

Slideshows
View images and captions

... and much, much more!

THRILLING SCIENCE AND TECHNOLOGY JOBS

ASTRONAUTS

Contents

AV2 Book Code	2
Just Another Day at Work	4
The International Space Station	6
Astronaut Training	8
Training for Zero Gravity	10
Welcome to the Space Station	12
Life on the Space Station	14
Sleeping, Running, and . . .	16
Astronaut Scientists at Work	18
A Human Experiment	20
Ready to Spacewalk	22
Walking in Space	24
The Journey Home	26
Welcome Back to Earth	28
Historic Space Missions	29
Astronaut Quiz	30
Key Words/Index	31

Just Another Day at Work

The countdown is over. A deafening roar bursts from the base of the Soyuz-FG rocket. As people around the world hold their breath, the rocket soars into the sky on a column of flame.

Blasting away from Earth are Timothy Kopra, Yuri Malenchenko, and Tim Peake. Just three scientists and **engineers** on their way to work!

In a few hours, the men will reach their destination—the International Space Station (ISS). Their training has been long and hard. But it will all be worth it to have the chance to live and work high above Earth in the most extreme **laboratory** ever built!

Soyuz-FG rockets blast off from the Baikonur Cosmodrome in Kazakhstan.

ISS Expedition 46 launched with crew members Timothy Kopra, Yuri Malenchenko, and Tim Peake on December 15, 2015.

As of 2019, more than **560 people** have traveled to space.

In 1998, astronaut John Glenn became the oldest person to travel to space at age **77**.

Russia's Yuri Gagarin was the **first person** in space.

Astronauts 5

The International Space Station

The International Space Station (ISS) is a workplace and home for up to six people. Aboard this space laboratory, astronauts and **cosmonauts** perform experiments that help us learn more about space travel and even life on Earth.

On a space station, everyday actions, such as getting a drink of water or going to the bathroom, are complex science problems. It has taken thousands of scientists and engineers many years to make life on the ISS possible by developing solutions to these problems.

The ISS **orbits** Earth 16 times in every 24-hour period. During each orbit, it moves into the Sun's light for 45 minutes and then into darkness for 45 minutes. This means the crew experiences 16 sunrises and 16 sunsets every day.

Watching their home planet is a favorite activity for the ISS crew.

ASTRONOMICAL

On Earth, **gravity** pulls everything, including us, down toward the ground. Inside the ISS or an orbiting spacecraft, everything experiences zero gravity and astronauts feel weightless.

Astronaut Training

Do you want to be an astronaut? When British pilot Tim Peake read the European Space Agency's (ESA's) advertisement, his answer was yes!

After beating more than 8,000 other applicants to get his dream job, Tim began six years of grueling astronaut training.

Astronauts on an ISS mission must learn every detail of how the space station works, and how to fix it if something goes wrong. A task that may take just one hour on the ISS will be practiced for hundreds of hours on Earth inside a **simulator**.

Astronauts study and prepare for the science experiments they will do in space. They also undergo medical training. When you are 250 miles (400 kilometers) above Earth, you cannot call a doctor. So all astronaut trainees learn procedures, such as giving shots, stitching up wounds, and helping someone who has stopped breathing.

During training, astronauts practice working as a team in extreme environments.

Where Astronauts Train

Scale: 0 — 250 miles / 402 kilometers

1 Johnson Space Center (JSC), Houston, Texas
The Johnson Space Center is NASA's main astronaut training center. Since 1961, JSC has trained more than 300 astronauts from around the world.

2 Sonny Carter Training Facility, Houston, Texas
The Neutral Buoyancy Laboratory is a giant water tank in the Sonny Carter Training Facility. Astronauts use it to practice working in zero gravity.

3 Kennedy Space Center, Titusville, Florida
In 2019, NASA astronauts at the Kennedy Space Center completed training off the coast of Florida to prepare for water landings.

Astronauts 9

Training for Zero Gravity

Time on the "Vomit Comet" is a must for every astronaut trainee!

To prepare for zero gravity in space, astronauts take training flights on a specially fitted aircraft. During a flight, the plane makes extreme climbs and dips. This creates zero gravity inside the plane for up to 25 seconds at a time. During the periods of weightlessness, astronauts practice moving around and doing tasks.

An astronaut may need to take part in an **Extravehicular Activity (EVA)** or "spacewalk" outside the ISS. Astronauts train for these highly dangerous missions underwater.

In a training pool, the feeling of being weightless is simulated. This allows astronauts to practice repairs and other tasks they will carry out during EVAs.

During training flights, astronauts practice using tools.

Astronaut

Support diver

Training pools contain mock-ups of objects such as the ISS.

ASTRONOMICAL

While underwater, astronauts wear a belt of heavy weights to make them sink and a suit filled with air to make them float. When the balance between sinking and floating is just right, an astronaut experiences a feeling that is similar to weightlessness.

Astronauts 11

Welcome to the Space Station

If the years of training are successful, an astronaut may one day be part of a crew hurtling away from Earth in a tiny *Soyuz* spacecraft.

It can take as little as six hours for the spacecraft to reach the ISS. Once the craft has **docked**, and a long list of checks is complete, the crew boards the space station.

Now that they are aboard the ISS, astronauts will neither feel nor taste fresh air for many months. The space station's Elektron system uses water, such as waste water from washing, to create breathable **oxygen**. The system separates **water molecules** into oxygen and hydrogen. The oxygen is pumped into the station for breathing. The hydrogen is vented, or released, into space.

A *Soyuz* spacecraft can carry three people, but it is a tight squeeze.

ASTRONOMICAL

As a theme park ride accelerates, you might be pushed back into your seat. The acceleration experienced by astronauts during a launch is a little like that—only it feels like a baby elephant is sitting on their lap!

At least one *Soyuz* spacecraft is docked with the ISS at all times.

Astronauts 13

Life on the Space Station

Aboard the ISS, water is precious. The crew uses as little as possible for washing up. They use "no rinse" shampoo that they simply comb through their hair. They also use edible toothpaste, so no water is wasted rinsing teeth.

All waste water on the ISS is recycled. Even the astronauts' urine is cleaned and recycled back into fresh drinking water.

Food aboard the ISS is specially developed to be long-lasting and crumb free. Crumbs might float away and **contaminate** equipment. Even salt and pepper are liquid. This stops tiny particles from clogging air vents or floating into an astronaut's eyes or nose.

When a supply spacecraft arrives from Earth, the ISS crew gets a delivery of fruit, vegetables, and other fresh foods.

A Meal on the ISS

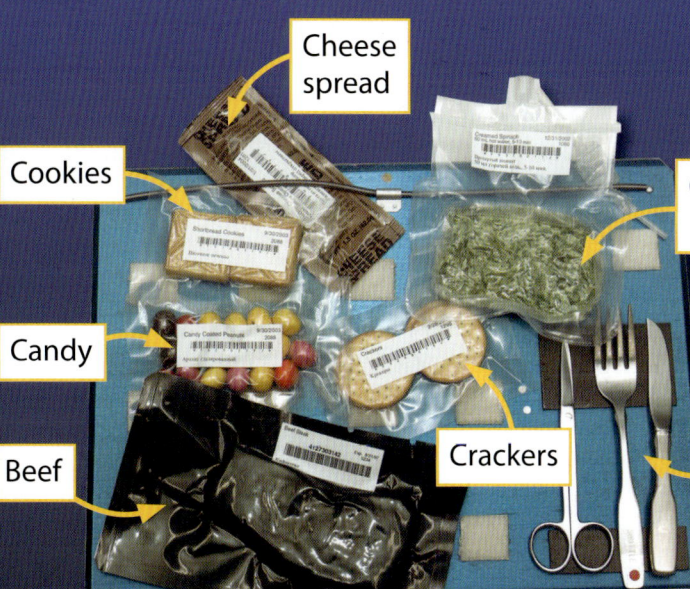

- Cheese spread
- Cookies
- Creamed spinach
- Candy
- Crackers
- Beef
- Cutlery attached to the tray with Velcro

In zero gravity, water and other liquids do not flow. Instead, they form into floating globules, or bubbles.

ASTRONOMICAL

Water is heavy, so it is not practical to send the water that astronauts need into space. Finding ways to recycle water aboard the ISS was a major challenge for the engineers and scientists who designed the space station.

Astronauts 15

Sleeping, Running, and ...

On the ISS, astronauts have to be neat or the air would be full of floating food, tools, and socks. Astronauts even sleep in sleeping bags anchored to the walls of their crew cabins.

Weightlessness makes an astronaut's muscles and bones grow weak. To keep their bodies strong, astronauts work out for two hours every day on the station's treadmill, stationary bike, and resistance equipment.

And the really big question?

When going to the bathroom, astronauts use a funnel attached to a pipe. Air then sucks the liquid away so it cannot escape. When sitting on the toilet, astronauts use seatbelt-like straps so they do not float off!

Astronauts using a treadmill on the ISS are strapped to the machine by bungee cords.

Astronauts relax by watching movies and playing games. Chess pieces are attached to the board by Velcro.

ASTRONOMICAL

On the ISS, urine is recycled into fresh water. For now, there is no use for other waste. A future scientific challenge is to find a way to recycle astronaut waste into something useful.

Astronauts 17

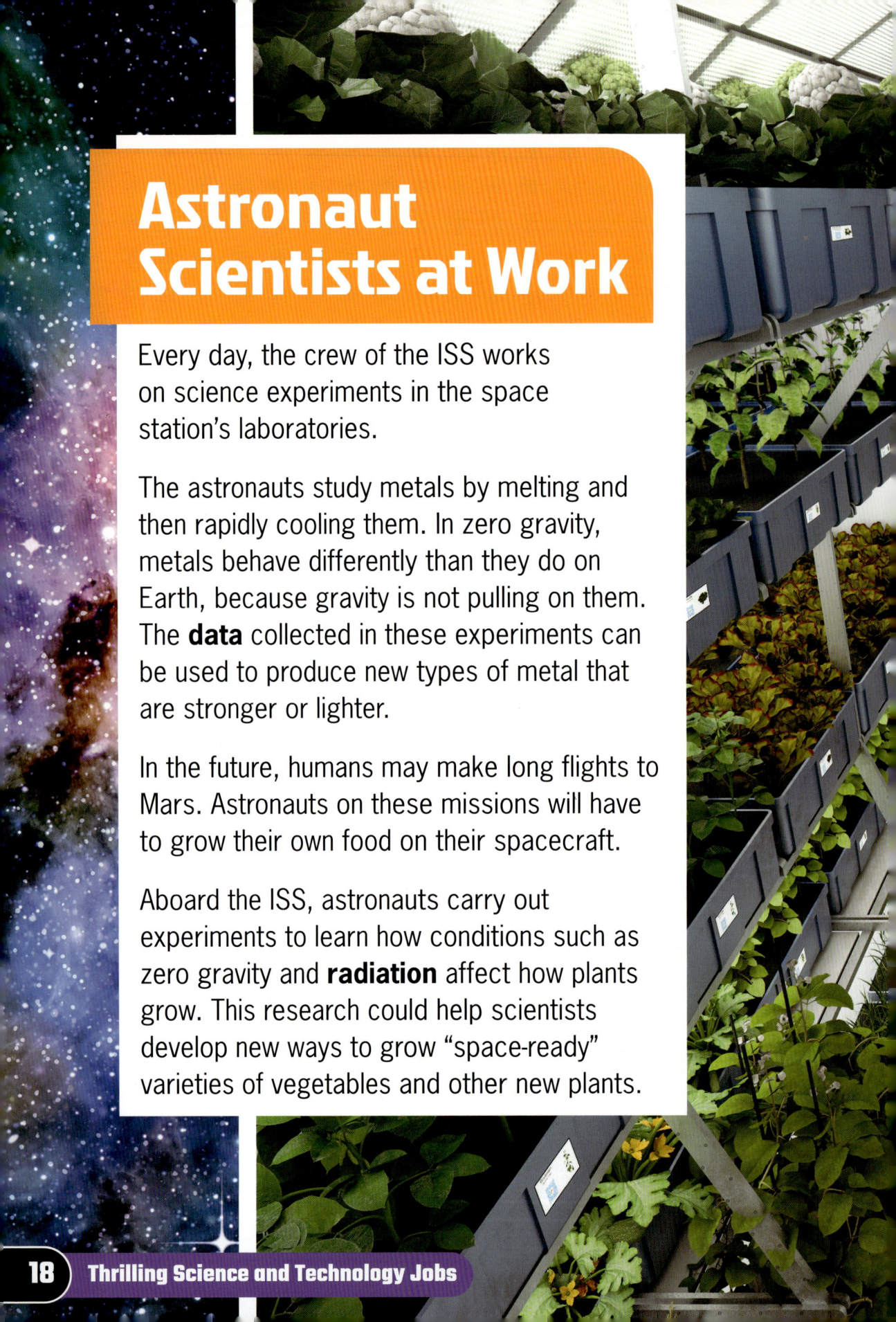

Astronaut Scientists at Work

Every day, the crew of the ISS works on science experiments in the space station's laboratories.

The astronauts study metals by melting and then rapidly cooling them. In zero gravity, metals behave differently than they do on Earth, because gravity is not pulling on them. The **data** collected in these experiments can be used to produce new types of metal that are stronger or lighter.

In the future, humans may make long flights to Mars. Astronauts on these missions will have to grow their own food on their spacecraft.

Aboard the ISS, astronauts carry out experiments to learn how conditions such as zero gravity and **radiation** affect how plants grow. This research could help scientists develop new ways to grow "space-ready" varieties of vegetables and other new plants.

Inside the ISS's Electromagnetic Levitator (EML), metals can be heated to 3,812°F (2,100°C).

Although none have been built yet, spacecraft in the future might have areas for growing plants such as beets, lettuce, tomatoes, zucchini, and beans.

ASTRONOMICAL

A new lightweight metal could be used to build cars or planes that will use less fuel. Vehicles that are more fuel efficient are better for the environment.

A Human Experiment

A mission to Mars and back could last for two years. How will living in space for that long affect an astronaut's body? Astronaut Scott Kelly actually became a human experiment to help answer that question.

Before Scott went to the ISS, he underwent extensive medical tests and examinations. After 340 days on the ISS, he returned to Earth to undergo further testing and monitoring.

Scott's twin brother Mark was also tested and examined. Mark, however, did not go into space.

Scientists studied the twins and compared them. This helped them learn in what ways the long stay in space affected Scott's body and health.

Scott and Mark both gave themselves flu shots. Scientists were able to investigate if being in space changed Scott's ability to fight off illnesses.

Scott Kelly took part in an experiment aboard the ISS to study how the body's fluids, such as blood, behave in zero gravity.

ASTRONOMICAL

During his mission, Scott monitored many parts of his body, including his eyes and heart. He also took samples from his body, such as blood and saliva. The samples were stored safely on the ISS so they could be analyzed back on Earth.

Astronauts 21

Ready to Spacewalk

The ultimate experience for any astronaut is to take part in an EVA, or spacewalk.

During a spacewalk, an astronaut wears a spacesuit called an Extravehicular Mobility Unit (EMU). Like a one-person spacecraft, an EMU supplies the astronaut with oxygen to breathe and water to drink. It also contains radio equipment to allow the astronaut to communicate with an EVA partner and the crew members still inside the ISS.

The astronauts put on their EMUs in a tiny room called an airlock. Once they are ready, the door that leads back into the space station is tightly closed. This keeps the air inside the space station from escaping. Then, the astronauts open the airlock's second door. This door leads out into the blackness of space.

A spacesuit's tough fabric protects an astronaut from tiny particles of space dust that can hit with the speed and power of a bullet.

The **first spacewalk** took place on March 18, 1965.

The first woman to perform a spacewalk was **Svetlana Savitskaya** in 1984.

It takes about **45 minutes** to put on a spacesuit.

Astronauts 23

Walking in Space

On January 15, 2016, astronauts Timothy Kopra and Tim Peake performed an EVA. The purpose of their mission was to replace a box of electronics on one of the station's huge **solar arrays**.

The two astronauts climbed almost to the opposite end of the station to the airlock door. Once they were in position, they waited for the ISS to move into darkness. With Earth blocking the Sun's light, they had just 30 minutes to replace the power unit. Once the ISS flew back into sunlight, high voltage electricity would surge through the electronics.

Working with tools such as a wrench and a pistol-grip screwdriver, they successfully replaced the power unit. It was a simple engineering task, but it was performed under the most dangerous and extreme conditions!

SAFER tether

SAFER jet pack

Astronauts use ropes, called safety tethers, to attach themselves to the station at all times. Without these tethers, they would float off into space.

ASTRONOMICAL

During an EVA, astronauts wear a jet pack called a Simplified Aid for EVA Rescue (SAFER). If a safety tether breaks or becomes unhooked, an astronaut can fly back to the ISS, controlling the jet pack with a small joystick.

The Journey Home

When a mission is over, the crew returns to Earth in their *Soyuz* spacecraft. The spacecraft undocks from the ISS and continues to orbit Earth. Then, about an hour before landing, the spacecraft makes a de-orbit burn. This slows it down and causes it to start falling back toward Earth.

At about 87 miles (140 km) above Earth's surface, the spacecraft separates into its three modules. Then, the tiny descent module containing the crew plunges into Earth's **atmosphere**, traveling at about 17,400 miles per hour (28,000 km/h).

Friction caused by air starts to slow the craft, and parachutes are deployed to reduce its speed. When it is about 5 miles (8 km) above Earth's surface, the craft's main parachute opens.

Main parachute

A *Soyuz* descent module's journey back to Earth takes just 3.5 hours.

Each seat in a *Soyuz* lander is specially designed to fit the person sitting in it.

ASTRONOMICAL

Once the descent module enters Earth's atmosphere, the crew experiences the force of Earth's gravity for the first time in months. Astronauts say their bodies begin to feel incredibly heavy. It is an effort just to lift their hands.

Welcome Back to Earth

The descent module is slowed by its parachute and by firing six rockets. Then . . . Bang. It hits the ground—hard!

Medical and rescue crews rush to the descent module and help the astronauts from their spacecraft. For the first time in months, the crew enjoys the taste and smell of fresh air. The astronauts are overjoyed to be home and will soon be reunited with their families. Their bodies, however, will take many months, and possibly years, to recover from their long stay in space.

One day, space scientists hope to send astronauts to Mars and perhaps beyond. The human body experiments underway on the ISS today will help make this goal a reality. So will the **pioneering** men and women who go to work on the space station.

After returning to Earth, an astronaut's body feels heavy as gravity causes blood to flow from the upper body back to the lower body.

Historic Space Missions

Humans first traveled to space more than 60 years ago. Since then, there have been many important missions undertaken by astronauts.

April 12, 1961 Cosmonaut Yuri Gagarin reaches space and orbits Earth once.

May 5, 1961 Astronaut Alan Shepard is the first U.S. astronaut in space.

1965 Cosmonaut Aleksey Leonov is the first person to take part in a space walk.

1969 Neil Armstrong and Edwin "Buzz" Aldrin are the first people to walk on the Moon.

1998 The first ISS modules are launched into space.

2000 Sergey Krikalyov, Yuri Gidzenko, William Shepherd are the first resident crew members onboard the ISS.

2009 The ISS becomes fully operational. Crews of six astronauts begin living in the station.

2019 Testing continues on SpaceX's Crew Dragon capsule, which will soon allow astronauts to reach the ISS from the United States.

Astronauts

Astronaut Quiz

01 Which astronaut twin stayed on Earth as part of a study?

02 What attaches astronauts on the ISS to their treadmill?

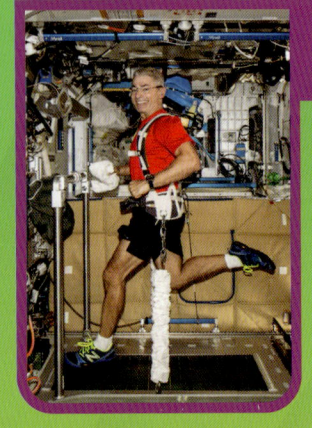

03 How long does a *Soyuz* descent module's journey back to Earth take?

04 What is a Simplified Aid for EVA Rescue (SAFER)?

05 When did the first spacewalk take place?

06 What to astronauts on the ISS use to avoid having to use water to rinse their mouths?

07 Do water and other liquids flow in space?

08 Who was the first person in space?

09 How long does it take a spacecraft to reach the ISS?

10 Who were the first people to walk on the Moon?

ANSWER
01 Mark Kelly **02** Bungee cords **03** 3.5 hours **04** A jetpack used during EVAs **05** March 18, 1965 **06** Edible toothpaste **07** No **08** Yuri Gagarin **09** As little as six hours **10** Neil Armstrong and Edwin "Buzz" Aldrin

30 Thrilling Science and Technology Jobs

Key Words

atmosphere: a layer of gases around a planet, moon, or star

contaminate: to harm or make something unclean by introducing something dirty or dangerous

cosmonauts: Russian astronauts

data: information and facts, often in the form of numbers

docked: securely connected to a space station or spacecraft

engineers: people who use math, science, and technology to design, build, and repair machines or structures

Extravehicular Activity (EVA): a spacewalk made by astronauts outside of the ISS or a spacecraft

gravity: the force that causes objects to be pulled toward other objects

laboratory: a room, building, or vehicle where there is equipment that can be used to carry out experiments and other scientific studies

orbits: when something circles, or moves around, another object

oxygen: an invisible gas in air that people and animals need to breathe

pioneering: the first to do something; leading the way

radiation: a type of invisible energy that travels through space. High levels of radiation can be harmful to living things.

simulator: a pretend version of something, such as a plane, spacecraft, or building

solar arrays: groups of solar panels joined together

water molecules: the smallest units of water, formed from two hydrogen atoms and one oxygen atom attached to each other

Index

ESA 8
EVAs (Extravehicular Activities) 10, 22, 24, 25, 30
experiments 6, 8, 18, 20, 28
food 14, 15, 16, 18, 19
gravity 7, 9, 10, 15, 18, 21, 28
Kelly, Mark 20, 30
Kelly, Scott 20, 21
Kopra, Timothy 4, 5, 24

laboratory 4, 6, 9, 18
launch 5, 13, 29

Malenchenko, Yuri 4, 5
Mars missions 18, 20, 28
NASA 9
oxygen 12, 22
Peake, Tim 4, 5, 8, 24
return to Earth 20, 26, 28

SAFER jet packs 25, 30
sleep 16
Soyuz spacecraft 4, 12, 13, 26, 27, 30
spacesuits 22, 23
training 4, 8, 9, 10, 11, 12
"Vomit Comet" 10
water 6, 9, 10, 11, 12, 14, 15, 17, 22, 30

Get the best of both worlds.

AV2 bridges the gap between print and digital.

The expandable resources toolbar enables quick access to content including **videos**, **audio**, **activities**, **weblinks**, **slideshows**, **quizzes**, and **key words**.

Animated videos make static images come alive.

Resource icons on each page help readers to further **explore key concepts**.

Published by AV2
350 5th Avenue, 59th Floor
New York, NY 10118
Website: www.av2books.com

Copyright © 2021 AV2
All rights reserved. No part of this publication may be reproduced, stored in a retrieval system, or transmitted in any form or by any means, electronic, mechanical, photocopying, recording, or otherwise, without the prior written permission of the publisher.

Library of Congress Control Number: 2019957559

ISBN 978-1-7911-2210-2 (hardcover)
ISBN 978-1-7911-2207-2 (softcover)
ISBN 978-1-7911-2208-9 (multi-user eBook)
ISBN 978-1-7911-2209-6 (single-user eBook)

Printed in Guangzhou, China
1 2 3 4 5 6 7 8 9 0 24 23 22 21 20

032020
101319

Project Coordinator: John Willis
Designer: Terry Paulhus

Every reasonable effort has been made to trace ownership and to obtain permission to reprint copyright material. The publishers would be pleased to have any errors or omissions brought to their attention so that they may be corrected in subsequent printings.

AV2 acknowledges Alamy, Getty Images, NASA, Shutterstock, and Wikimedia as its primary image suppliers for this title.

First published in 2017 by Ruby Tuesday Books Ltd.